OLIVER CROMWELL

by Fergus Dowding

THE HELLIDON PRESS

CATESBY END, HELLIDON

NORTHAMPTONSHIRE NN11 6GB

Monkey business

OLIVER Cromwell was born a citizen of the country town of Huntingdon in 1599. By the time he died nearly sixty years later in 1658, he was Lord Protector of England - King in all but name and one of the most famous men in England's history.

Oliver grew up with a strong sense of justice, great courage and self-confidence. When there was wide unhappiness with the way King Charles I was ruling the country, Oliver could have retired to his farm and lived the comfortable life of a gentleman farmer, but he did not. Cromwell fought to see justice done and changed the government of England forever.

There is a tale of an early adventure in Cromwell's life. It took place at Hinchinbrooke Hall, the home of Oliver's grandfather Sir Henry Cromwell. Sir Henry spent all his money on a fabulous lifestyle. He was known locally as 'the Golden Knight' and kept a magnificent household that included a pet monkey. One day this monkey playfully ran onto the roof of the house with the newly born Oliver in his mouth. Just imagine what his mother thought when she saw the scene!

An ominous quarrel

THERE is another more prophetic story told of when the future King Charles I and Cromwell first met. The then King of England, James I visited 'the Golden Knight' at Hinchinbrooke Hall together with his young son, Prince Charles. There were important affairs to discuss so the two young boys were sent out into the garden to play. The boys quarrelled and fought, and Oliver was the winner. Little did anyone know that this story was to be re-enacted years later on a huge scale, with both men having an army at his back.

Oliver had six sisters but no brothers. He went to the local school in Huntingdon where he learnt to mix and play with other boys. He went on to university at Cambridge, but while he was there his father died. As he was the only man in the family, he returned home to support his mother and six sisters. Their life was a comfortable one. They were neither rich nor poor, but by working hard on the farm they could afford to live well.

Oliver was intelligent and ambitious and soon he began to take an interest in national affairs. Fate was about to propel him into the history books.

Opposition

AT the age of twenty nine, Cromwell was elected to the House of Commons as the Member of Parliament for Huntingdon. Parliament at this time was a stormy affair and on Oliver's first day he witnessed a shocking scene.

Parliament is only allowed to conduct business when the Speaker is sitting on the Woolsack. This is literally a sack of wool and was first introduced in the fourteenth century when wool was the foundation of England's wealth. The Speaker still sits on the Woolsack today, over seven hundred and fifty years after it was first used.

The Speaker on this day was a friend of King Charles. A Member of Parliament called John Eliot wanted to make various complaints about the way the King was running the country, especially regarding the high taxes that the King had imposed without bothering to consult Parliament. The Speaker tried to stand up so that Eliot could not speak, but tempers were running high and the Speaker was roughly held on the Woolsack while Eliot had his say.

King Charles immediately dissolved Parliament. It was to be eleven years before Parliament again met at Westminster. During that time many people grew to hate and mistrust the King.

A rough way to run a country. But worse was to come.

The Puritans

IN the seventeenth century there was a large and fanatical religious sect called the Puritans. The name was given to them because they wanted to 'purify' church services by making them much simpler. They hated statues, paintings and music in church, preferring plain whitewashed walls so as not to distract the mind from praying. They lived quiet and humble lives. They felt that people should not indulge in parties - no drinking, singing, dancing and music of any sort. Puritan dress was simple and sober - no lively colours and frills for them. Of course, not all the Puritans were as severe as those on the opposite page. It was only a very few who thought you had to be constantly gloomy to be good!

Cromwell was a Puritan, although a mild one. King Charles was the very opposite of a Puritan. He loved fine clothes and extravagant parties. He was also suspected by many of supporting the Roman Catholic church which was very unpopular in England at the time.

The Puritans were very influential in Parliament and in the forthcoming civil war they were able to act on their religious beliefs. Church choirs were disbanded and thousands of religious statues and objects were destroyed. Cromwell himself dismissed the congregation of Ely Cathedral during the service and the Cathedral remained closed for the following seventeen years. However this was all in the future.

Rumblings of discontent

ENGLAND was not a happy place during the eleven long years that the King governed without Parliament. The root of the problem was that King Charles I believed in 'the divine right of Kings'. This was an old belief that meant a King was answerable only to God. This allowed him to rule his kingdom as he liked, never having to ask for advice because God was ruling through him. Why then did he have to suffer the inconvenience of a Parliament? If he needed more money, then taxes had to be increased. It was God's will.

Sadly for Charles, Parliament and the rest of the country did not believe in this divine right to rule. Riots broke out up and down the country in protest at the ever-increasing and illegal tax burden.

Cromwell himself very nearly lost his farm. The land around St Ives in Lincolnshire was very wet and boggy, but when drained made very good farming land. The King proposed to drain the land using money from public funds. This was a good idea except he then intended to give the land to the Bedford family who were his very good friends!

One man, William Prynne, published a pamphlet attacking the King and his wife, Queen Henrietta Maria. He was captured, fined, pilloried and was to have his ears cut off. Crowds gathered to show their anger at Prynne's treatment and he was released. Prynne did not give up and printed more angry pamphlets. He was eventually branded on the cheek with a red hot iron with the initials SL for Seditious Libeller. Poor man!

Civil war

THINGS went from bad to worse for King Charles and eventually he had to recall Parliament because he simply could not raise enough money to run the country despite his unpopular and illegal taxes.

Parliament drew up a document called the 'Grand Remonstrance.' This was a list of grievances with the King, which asked that he only use Ministers appointed by Parliament to run the country. Some Members of Parliament thought this was out of order and sided with the King. But many of the MPs were adamant that these grievances were justified. Furious debates took place in the House and the King's patience finally snapped in January 1642. Taking some soldiers with him, the King went to the Houses of Parliament to arrest five of the rebellious MPs. They heard he was coming and fled the House. When Charles saw they had gone, he made his now famous remark, "I see all the birds have flown."

The King returned to his palace determined to get his way by force if necessary. Parliament was equally determined. War between the two was unavoidable.

Cavaliers and Roundheads

KING Charles left London, never to return until seven years later as a prisoner. He raised his standard at Nottingham and the English Civil War began.

The terrible tragedy of Civil War is that it divides the country - Englishmen fighting Englishmen, friends fighting friends and brothers fighting brothers. Everyone in the country had to decide who to support, either Parliament or the King, and so became sworn enemies of the other.

Most of the North and West of the country took the King's side. London, the Midlands and East Anglia followed Parliament. Each side tried to find as many soldiers as it could. There was a short-lived fashion for Puritans to cut their hair very short, so Parliament's troops were nicknamed Roundheads.

The King's supporters were called Cavaliers, an Italian word for horseman, because most of the King's men were wealthy and could afford to ride horses.

The first major battle of the war at Edgehill in Warwickshire was largely indecisive, but Captain Cromwell proved himself a natural military leader. He was interested in his men and treated them fairly but trained them with iron discipline. Because of this discipline they were soon known as 'Ironsides'. Cromwell was soon promoted to the rank of Lieutenant-General.

Marston Moor

THE battle of Marston Moor in Yorkshire was the biggest of the Civil War

Each side formed a line one and a half miles long on the edge of a moor close to York. The Royalist army was led by Prince Rupert of the Rhine, a nephew of King Charles, and a true cavalier in the romantic sense of the word. He was young, handsome and 'very sparkish' in dress. It was seven o'clock on a wet July evening by the time the two armies were in place. Rupert assumed the battle would start the following morning and went off to eat his dinner.

Parliament seized the opportunity to attack. Lieutenant-General Cromwell's cavalry made a deliberately slow but sure charge on the right flank, a daring move which would normally have been cut to pieces by musket fire from the Royalist infantry. But the Royalist cavalry could not resist charging straight at Cromwell, thereby obstructing their own musket fire. There was now a grim fight, sword against sword, with many casualties on both sides. However, Cromwell's Ironsides kept their formation and eventually won the engagement.

Meanwhile, Parliament's centre and left flanks were being overwhelmed by the courage and tenacity of the Royalist attack. It looked as if the Royalists would win the day. But in the nick of time Cromwell, with characteristic speed and courage, turned his Ironsides round and attacked the Royalist centre from behind. The King's army stood and fought like men to the last. Only thirty men out of two thousand survived in the centre. By nightfall the battle was over and Oliver Cromwell had won

A midnight arrest

THE battle of Marston Moor was conclusive; Parliament was now winning the war. Cromwell did not rest. He managed to steer a Bill through Parliament which made all army commanders offer their resignation. Only the most hard-working and clever commanders were re-appointed and the famous 'New Model Army' was created. This consisted of twenty two thousand men at a cost of six thousand pounds a month. It truly was a model army, its well-disciplined and organised soldiers were well supplied, had a high morale and could be relied upon. This was put into good effect in 1645 at the Battle of Naseby in Northamptonshire, the last great battle of the Civil War. The Royalists were routed.

In April 1646 Charles was surrounded at Oxford. He managed to escape disguised as a servant and got as far as Newark in Nottinghamshire. Here, he surrendered himself to the Scottish army. The Scots soon found, as Parliament had found before them, that Charles was not to be trusted and sold him to Parliament for four hundred thousand pounds.

King Charles was taken to Holdenby House in Northamptonshire under house arrest, but arguments soon broke out between Parliament and the New Model Army about what to do next. Cromwell decided that it would be best if the King was held by him and his soldiers.

At midnight, an officer named Joyce rode to Holdenby House and demanded the surrender of the King. When the Parliament guards asked by what authority, Joyce drew his pistol and replied 'By this.'

Death of a monarch

CROMWELL was by now respected as the most able General in the army. He wished to see Charles re-instated as King but with restricted powers, and Parliament governing the country - much like the monarchy today. Charles, as untrustworthy as ever, talked at length with Cromwell but was also secretly negotiating with France and Scotland to help him overthrow Parliament.

At last, even Cromwell realised that whatever promises Charles made would never be kept and reluctantly agreed for the King to be tried before a Court at Westminster. He was charged as a tyrant and as one who had caused the death of thousands in the Civil War. On the 20th January 1649 Charles was found guilty. Ten days later on a bitterly cold and snowy morning at Whitehall Palace, Charles bent his head onto the block. A minute later the executioner, a man called Brandon, held up the severed head with the cry "Behold the head of a traitor."

There was no cheering from the watching troops. Instead a great groan was heard. Perhaps it was necessary to execute King Charles but it could never be said to be right.

But who was to rule the country now?

Lord Protector of England

PARLIAMENT tried to rule the country by itself but argued ceaselessly and to such an extent that nothing was achieved. Cromwell realised that a leader was needed if the country was to avoid slipping into a state of anarchy. In 1653 just as the King had done eleven long years ago, Cromwell marched into the House of Commons with a regiment of soldiers and dissolved Parliament with the words 'Get you gone and give place to honest men'. Cromwell was now supreme ruler of the republic of England.

Cromwell was offered the throne by a later Parliament, but refused to accept it. Instead he became The Lord Protector of England and governed the country well and fairly with one exception. The Irish remained loyal to the monarchy and were prepared to fight for Charles II, the son of King Charles I. Cromwell crossed to Ireland with an army to crush all resistance. The Irish were no match for the experienced Ironsides. The towns of Drogheda and Wexford were quickly captured and all the defenders were ruthlessly killed. To this day the 'Curse of Cromwell' is remembered.

Oliver Cromwell died peacefully in 1658. He was a good man who had helped save his country from the tyranny of a foolish King. He was deeply religious and - apart from in Ireland - fair and never cruel. His body was not allowed to rest in peace however. Two years after his death, when Charles II was on the throne, Cromwell's corpse was dug up and his head put on a spike. The irony of it all was that the order for this barbarous act had come from Parliament.

ACKNOWLEDGEMENTS

The publishers would like to thank Ladybird Books Ltd for permission to reproduce all the colour illustrations in this book and Elena Christie for kindly reading the text.

Published by the Hellidon Press. 01327 263852